PETER RICHARDS

HELSINKI

ACTION BOOKS
NOTRE DAME, IN
2011

ACTION BOOKS

EDITORS: Joyelle McSweeney & Johannes Göransson
ART DIRECTION: Jesper Göransson & Eli Queen
WEB DESIGN & EDITORIAL: John Dermot Wood
EDITORIAL ASSISTANT: Kimberly Koga
BOOK DESIGN: Bobby McKenna

Action Books gratefully acknowledges the support of the College of Arts and Letters at the University of Notre Dame.

Action Books
Department of English
University of Notre Dame
356 O'Shaughnessy Hall
Notre Dame, IN 46544

Visit us online at actionbooks.org.

Helsinki
ISBN 978-0-979-9755-9-2
Library of Congress Control Number: 2010938272

FIRST EDITION

F O R   B I N D U

HELSINKI

1

+ + +

In time I came to see death was the hay
binding one soldier to another and my own
death would appear partially lit as during
a nighttime operation the moon barely attends
whereas I with new density carry on as before
again I go razing Tanagra so plainly familiar
to me that it does sit upon my own reflection
and all about me on deck where my double
does well so the spoils and I can finally make
it just this or that way for a while never mind
the snipers the charges and this loose cloud
of animal gadgetry eating air and chrome alike
until absent any ship garrison or wish to remain
we set out with our lancets on idle command

+ + +

When we came upon this large orange hide
staked to the ground by three orange feathers
I knew one of our boys lay headless beneath it
but from the air who could tell he was one
of my own or that I would come to remember
his face what restraint he brought to my tent
at night his anxiety that seemed to smile upon
me same way a white dot begins to ripen inside
this one mountain of Nice a face of sad orange
decorative stone where I lay surviving the prattle
but losing the kiss until finally I gave his name
to the mountain the campaign all night the full
story how for sixteen hours I hung from the beams
of the parliament ceiling and while the jeering
population looked on I could hear in the blackout
the plan for one day holding their lives in my hand

+ + +

Possibly a human face grows intensely black
when excited for I was carried inside a blackened
little ship of playing fields and hives involving
practical guides to civilization in the white dot's
presence I felt this ongoing chance to be neglected
I was being photographed by a flag of especially
crying six-thousand men each one having deserted
the patriotic part of a lion for now on they study
my life as a papal state and consider it my duty
to maintain a forcibly shaved militia between two
families there's a ball we can touch together during
the party one of the oarsmen rolled me a cigarette
when he stood up I could see his waist was enchanted

+ + +

He wore a tight aqua t-shirt which signifies
to me at least the end of June actually
the whole of March bears out in a reasonable
way my recollections of a well known cellist
still playing at home her mat was made of horsehair
her mat was made of green horse feathers
and much to her disgust I sometimes wore
my uniform and sometimes bit her seneca lobe
which has every appearance of being modern
and contrite but contains the initial error
I sometimes see behind Mohammedan curtains
or the magazine said to contain 70 of the world's
most beautiful men they seem timid at first
but just start in with a little Portuguese and you
will soon find no man is a better authority than
any other man any divinity as the low end estimate
of a number some arbiters regard as a trick for it does
not record the fact nor contain action requiring
thought in clear view my recent attempt was like
my first in that I neither consulted the highest
nor was I ever truly released from Helsinki

+ + +

I do remember as a small boy being brushed
by a black man in the courtyard feeling the small
of my back lightly brushed so that it sank deep
into my imagination and partly the initial deathblow
Helsinki prepared for my boyhood drawing an invisible
orange line at the base of my skull leading to this villa
my parents shared between them each room holding
a portrait of one of my parts and one room wrongly
represents the cyst in my knee another captures my chin
before it was mended a third stretches to the evil side
of the room where this tear sits hard and white and so
I think it must be cold so cold the cold outnumbers ice
from when the ice was young no tear has taken its place
so it must live beyond the great doors of winter and sing
as many flesh and blood songs as a frozen tear can sing

+ + +

Providing these consultations
remain unsaid if he kissed me
he kissed me in fugitive droves
and disappearing were the soldiers
surrounding us both except they
were ably and frank and as soon
as undone he refused to do other
man's bidding knowing our night
made for that negative evidence
compared to his eyes lesser black
was the lozenge shouting disinterest
in the ship in its spatial authority
some other being must have left
open and in places wantonly split

+ + +

My tube was never removed so this painting depicts
the continuation of sound passing through one boundary
wall to the next on and out into space where I still have
a more or less decent view of the villa though it looks small
and perversely flat and pink like a tile or patch of laminated
foil on the head of a rat still it seems fairly represented and I
can still make out a little bit of me huffing in the wrongly placed
foreground where there is no eyewitness save for the disordered
fellow himself I suspect to be overwritten and miserably white
inside his chamber even the spirit of the hour won't convulse
in his bed fatalist to excess he uses small bodies and forgetfulness

+ + +

I myself forget how my death was privately tended
it lasted about three minutes I awoke in a villa
to the sensation gently brushing my back I could see
his face looking down at me through masses of hair
then we started quarreling I don't know something
malpractice or shirts until gradually I was no longer free
or prevented from seeing his face the locus for innumerable
variants ELDERS VOLUME RUG POUTING MUSCATELS
I mean the variants were everywhere and they went on
forever even my first step was drawn from his face
but that I myself was rumor and whether or not we actually
went together I leave for you to decide because I don't really
want to talk about that anymore not here anyways
where I can honestly say I know what it feels like to be
roasted forever on green spits in a cool halted valley
of repeating presence where no weather is the kingdom itself

+ + +

My own bad recollection landed me too much alive
to the first signs of disintegration in a prairie in a baby
metabolizing bees was the first sign my illness had presented
the feminine smells of devisable matter and sheer overjoy
exploring the hindquarters of an ox and all the flash clubs
in Helsinki had the foresight to be in Helsinki everywhere
these huge constant moth wings beat out applause
from a resolute childless population the impossible costumes
disembark and climb down from the rock face without
appearing neutral I retreat like an oaf to where there is no
place to get to and all these heavy lidded numbers and all
these enthusiasts watching me cry and I was in no way part
of your studio time I was alive I had a smooth bronze
forehead feeling partially at ease in the fist of loving people
or enjoying a gallant walk about town or volunteering
with a smile to let down my hair but tonight I can hear
the worms detonate tonight the worms perusing our scales

+ + +

I came to that underground field
each aspect appears on the blades
it's one of the qualities underground
we each appear indelible visible
precisely as ourselves but in the way
letters in a name might come oddly
assorted I never fully wore the skin
of my name as when seeing my name
pass in that way forever staring down
a black perfect candle all things
good health and blight
the wind unchanging in stillness
spat out a flame spat out each aspect
or I never did put on steam clothing
crushed with love by the Caspian Sea

+ + +

I came upon this handsome older man
his head was crawling with loam and minotaur lice
he asked me to be his life size effigy to apprehension
his back was dripping with three bickering lashes
and so full like an orange torn open
or a washboard for washing meat
his eyes looked inward blank disquieting slots
or steam clotted drains where the hemispheres
do war and the hemispheres unite
your waters are too swirled and justifiable
for me to go with you right now
I need more time no I need some time first
days of pure hand holding and lots of chats
completely free of anabasis and long dinners
where I can serenely drink from your back
maybe then we could be more than just friends
with lots of fun jaunts and SHUT THE FUCK UP
he said pulling my braid not so hard that it came
free of my head but hard enough that I was pulled
face down into his lap not like the lap of a choir
or the officer's lap or Julia's lap or even that lap on a track
when the racing is through it's true there were times
in life when I threw some races the money was good
but I hardly see how that fits with this I mean
isn't there another less severe SHUT THE FUCK UP
this time he hissed and this time the braid came free
of my head and without looking back I looked
back to see the old man twining my braid

in his four-hundred fingers palsy I shouted
PUNSTER he yelled and with that we both had
a good laugh and you should have been with us
that day when we all went sledding together
down a great monster of sunlight and hair

+ + +

By the time we reached the stable it was that time
of year when the sun wobbles free of its namesake
and reclines fully clothed on its late northern sofa
when embers convalescing in heaps echo the colors
too happy to share the first outer lips of the trees
blasting in their speech tells a cautionary tale
ending in ice and ice in all its final say
sentences each mimic to the blue voids on a robe
such is my howitzer as I scan the world's precedent
for moods form and changing shape each slow
falling gavel and spiraling decree nothing can be
numerated by any commission endless architecture
clips barbs latches and spires even the separate atoms
woe to be counted when a mountain with so many
unburdens itself hearing cries from the buried ones
failing inside a mouth clogged with it recalls my own
failure to ever capture in words the whitened season

//

+ + +

She came previous to herself and knocks
those things in ignorance I spoke about
questioning if she were the ghost at play
in my dream and pressing leaves in a book
so that I could observe them not shattering
aging beautifully knowing they were oak
leaves touching on violet but also tinges
of falconry brown the hood that is or glove
though by royal decree not the same leather
for the hood there is thought to be endless
with its own stars sanctums and fragrance
a darkness that collects on the finger
in thick green spirals of harrowing shade

+ + +

My leader trailing off into reels
lethargy and hair I could see
between the toing and the froing
a plume of green winged horses
each no bigger than a bee
and the sound of their industry
rhymes with the star-swath I held
as a child for all its spherical depth
I wondered if it wasn't the gaze
from so many others passing as a
wink from one system to the next
on and on and forever the accretion
until all of us are here together
and the shared hush from our looking
is all that I ask the heavens to bring

+ + +

But it is one thing to ask and another to hope whispered one
this devisable one astray from the virescent herd and though
equestrian in all things shape and manner she appeared more
as a hummingbird than a hummingbird could be and so bright
was the sheen on her feathers it required the same shuttered
glances when the eye takes joy in the sun enduring the moon
or when the sun bath-salt of the evening pink orange blue
stammering yokes or that one summer teaching esl to a field
of modern dancers the sheen from her feathers is a flame she can
pass through and as she sat there exquisitely preening on my finger
I could say she was an extraordinarily practical green flying horse
such was the thrift by which she enjoyed warming her body
at the hearth of its own luminosity and the circles she made
on my finger in all their tidings cadence and joy why it felt like
matrimony itself but without the chronic ceremony she began
to undress herself first came the bridle then helmet then lacing
the saddle made of true clergymen leather and Greek molecular
systems set in huge sounding garnets rounding the horn sliding
out from her the saddle fell to the ground looking less like a saddle
than a gold foil throne full of sunshine gossip and green shouting dew

+ + +

There is a place in Helsinki called Timocharis
with baleful hills and baleful ditches but speak
of that place when you get to it because next
came her shoes well but not exactly like shoes
horses wear on Earth for one was named Julia
and as it came free of her hoof it too sprouted
wings from its own iridescence and like a naked
girl endlessly climbing a horse so Julia climbed
upon it and when finally the other shoe fell it
fell namelessly into my hand where it was called
THE GIN FOR REPEATING HANDS each hand
repeating the other I held Julia for a kingdom
my hand a lather of hands and so innumerable
were the hands and the cooing they made together
itself a kind of mechanism for it brought new
rules of engagement not only between horse person
and shoe but also WOULD YOU PLEASE GO TO SLEEP
whispered Julia almost asleep on her horse
who was also nearly sleeping and hovering away
from my hand she left me this little pile of green
light to look at and smell and use as a guide

+ + +

What do you suppose behind all that netting
each eyelet attacking your two red pawns
tending winter coming alive serving up blood
crushing a city for a white dot the norths can
enjoy breaking apart an orange choirless pill
the first half going down with the next perfect
in time until all I could hear was the netting
making primeval noises one breast nudging
the other I cannot read from their vantage
a lamp signals YES YES measure us completely
just leaning over they appear not to weigh
as I imagined they would on purpose withholding
news of our total exertion do they sometimes
practice like that blazing in soap or do they keep
their elations mostly at bay I don't know from
pretending one breast can outstare the other

+ + +

It feels like I'm dripping down a very large flower
it's the lamp it's the odor black straps composing
my face once as you were leaning over I traveled
to some bad foreseeable depths all taste completely
hidden lengthwise indulged and the great dreck shape
rearing listless punctual and all so broken apart
barking out orders to the shapes it delays but never
at you for all Helsinki could not shout to the wonder
in daylight when you just walked away swinging those
huge and living absolute gongs and my own dated
circle is not once to have seen them crowning the air

+ + +

Julia bellows what now had become the most
refined tract of her patience and gathers
herself behind a massive pill she had otherwise
taken from the dead a mixture of fame and cattle
seldom gave her a speckled urn containing humidity
from sex to sex as if coves could maintain a likeness
to themselves or that below sea the same things do
occur before that she was somewhat divided and can
no longer endure seeing a man being seated nor
the matters of a household set out among the lawns
of summer before that Christ had risen so that nothing
reasonably ladylike could exist not smoldering May poles
in the stars breasts in heaven have this terrible symmetry
not there in the day nor in the night they wash up perfectly
betraying the outlines of clap and hoof beneath a plain
number three in the middle of a square the hoarfrost seems
like grieving in space slow quick and at the same time each
hand is a hand among people in the old days baying old

+ + +

In the extreme she began to suspect
each place in the world was planted
in meat and allowed to grow to a height
of eight or nine inches then removed
from its element and washed free
of its particles and continuously
polished with the same ease enjoyed
by the past a place can be removed
from the hand and placed laterally
over a pathway for closer study keeps
standards outside of time and for a while
held upright pressing lightly at the base
SOCIETY IS PREVENTED BY PAINTING
THE OUTER LIPS BLACK in this way
it become possible to follow Julia
to the last formation of land increasing
in size I was adopted for the study

+ + +

In the round without escort I kneel inside the plume
it seems like that elk I feed in the dream my head
not yet mangled with switches or the dream where I sleep
in the lap of a choir or Julia's first nakedness recorded
as smell what seems grows vexed spiny and with the first
true colors of fire with the tediums fire lends to itself
to shade the suffering aspect is how continuously the first
colors surrender their names in shade colors fall away
like a folio combusting with names from the mouth
of the shade came sighs dislodging the ledge I did not
wish to hear from the mouth of the shade these frayed
transom of ledges until commodious and together mouth
and fire made chimney of the marriage IN THIS PART OF LIFE
WE CAN SEE YOU'VE ALREADY CONSENTED IN THIS PART
OF LIFE WE CAN SEE YOU FOREVER HUNCHED OVER AND WITH
THE PRE-SHIVERING OF HAIR STICKING TO MEAT when the shade
finally slumped saddened BUT I SHOULDN'T BE SPEAKING
a gray plume gradations of plume lay smoldering there on the path
and as one who shouldn't be speaking I saw how I should not
speak to this place and proceeded downward as twilight mute
twilight distending the circles

+ + +

People open to combing seem truly ventilated
and closing their eyes it usually happens
the fears combs have of people are barely real
though often they evolve as fears and seem
dependent on unhappy campaigns of punishment
when a comb denied the rights of command gets
held in a manner inconsistent with the wishing
combs are just normal people in the atmosphere
raking the air for air cannot say it gentle enough

+ + +

Derived from earth spray dress code and Erheart's
fog forming galleons leave the sunshine in Helsinki
feeling strapless and underpaid and happy like a week
old rabbit that can speak but only to say will you rub
me I'm an x-rayed bale of hay if the shine is discreet
guileless and full of advice like the light from this analogy
leaving sprigs of semen in your hair and forcing us both
to say it's all the same roughly combed light to me anyways
it will not speak so I comb it I comb it I comb it comb it
comb it that's enough plainly you're pressing down too
hard I want to go please you're hurting me it hurts

+ + +

Send also occasional nubs and hand holding
people because each hurt is a real room
in a real villa and not like a hurt in the world
one might actually trust but more like a hurt
saying would that I was only this hurt we could
have gone on living behind one of those days

+ + +

When I came to it was a place impossible
to distinguish from the place in my sleep
and so severe was the damage to my sleep
I could see a great mistake had been made
to have slept there at all and how damaging
it was to the hand in the dream should I lay
in that hand and should the shingles believe
me as though all learning truly is recollection
a sash working a tournament trails through
one cataracting room to the next for there are
no paintings really only static land-based projects
towing executive hair and fully robed statues
preexisting their quarries and spending more
and more time alone in the villa I can barely
recall this honeycombed ridge what was it doing
mouthing characteristics of its own terrain
inklings my taste had gotten used to full-truck
sunsets oars made of thickening glass and sudden
postponements the sensation being featly carried
inside a whitened swat of applauding spheres
voyages where each man can bring his own hug
the ditch where I saw a mainsail completing itself

+ + +

Exactly which part of me did boiling a hammer
not intend to say and running up to a bridge
without even asking and the sudden ceiling
the officer drew me in his likeness he drew me
his pistol and asked me to wear it and possibly
being raised by true talking sisters and stopping
to watch three show-me state dancers working
the banquet hall from three-tiered coaches of air
in another life I disgraced my uniform by helping
them murder a priest and carving fierce looking
figures from my ovoid slum and wandering around
in the testimony of tropical air I soon distinguished
myself from those pigs you can see in the paintings
by taking six tallish brutes whose nudity was their art

+ + +

In heaven a light heart I was their tall sunbathing
leader and if I often did affect one serving his leader
my diet consisted mainly of poi and some 400
university suppers and if I often did amuse myself
demanding discipline from a poorly trained dancer
she trolls about the village with this new argument
to her hair and planting brains in the yard she built
me this bench where superficial greetings are made
wishes submitted and half-praising complaints
flexing in starlight and if they wrapped me in a thick
guava sheet the bats were landing there and together
on the island my dog and I look around and the slights
and the people of tall grasses sitting carelessly at my feet
and all the ocean was given to me a single black shiny
violet a moustache falling loosely to my neck and totems
they grant me their happy fatigue preceding middle height
and that universal oval face lowered like a grill onto a face
set free in the ventricle of a comet where indeed I was
blasted and conspicuous and white

+ + +

Between autumn and spring I sleep inside a column
streaming semen from the sky the time for mapping
and counting is done and it feels really good
just letting the waves make their own history
appearing only to myself in the ice pack not clocking
a waterway or a seamstress or discussing with a wren
her own innate sentence probably there exists bright
visual ones reared during previous causes especially
on occasion if we all pulse together crowds can confuse
them leaving unused tags floating in the den but some
of them how do they know a short time will suffice
how can they be put down and discriminate absolute
shape from color-form sources after a long season appearing
only to myself in the ice I feel like the wrong people
are burning bright visual ones appearing outside the body
eating by myself seems to be the most important task
for it suggests there may be more than one of us either
newly buried or drilling alone in the lard quiet

+ + +

Inside I saw what looked to be hair floating
about three prisms put forward I was a white
strand open at both ends one cell to the next
food overhead in a locker there the observers
they resemble Christ's two punctured heads
sipping a fugue in place of their sun the words
sit nearly taken OUR SUN GAVE WAY ALL ITS
INFORMATION a narrow slit no particular stripe
a birthright give it a chance I can turn by myself
I'm showing them my direction distance leaves
an upsetting pattern a fragrance to be attended
I lie in the arms of complete whiteness
a rope feeds into me moving up and down
I'm an orange foaming corset making occasions
REFERENCE THE GROUND I make gold partial
directionless rings and underpin sounds
and memories the bay state operation sideshow
shovel some blue jays of course I'm connected
I got orientation patterns a compound eye
more than one entrance at the start of a journey
I see flowers and narrow migration windows
come with me come point directly at a flower
you're a guide you have patterns inside you
frequently you arrive you create access you survive
you leave plenty of outline you attract me invisible
agrees with paper find water be visitors send each
other more MORE competing bodies is what it needs

+ + +

How did I actually become one of them
choosing polar quarters is one thing I mean
I'm hardly moving here unruffled by the waves
still I do feel other times might exist or at least
another clearing of equal deviation the animals
seem familiar contiguous and at the same time
my column stretches over a range about nine times
the normal range and released at the center of the clearing
gradually there should be no tapping for five days
no interruptions no captures a few wild ones finding
their way back if I could just carry one and release it
to a place very faithful laid in light growing older
it moves about in the attitudes as another direction
THE WHITENED SKY yes but I just want to see one
sleeping fathoms away from where it was done

+ + +

Before Julia turned maiden
she brought one of her sisters
to the resting motion school
there I was finally conceived
and rejoice never having been
frozen obstinate singing No
to the tradition where death
opens a kingdom

+ + +

THE SUBJECT LEAVES A WHITE PRODIGIOUS COLOR

yes I accept it

the subject leaves a white prodigious color

APPREHENDED BY A RAILING

I accept it

the subject was apprehended by a railing

THAT WHICH IS NOT A RAIL IS NOT A COLOR

APPREHENDED WE CIRCLE IT

WHITENED AND WITH THE RAIL MAKING

HARMONIES SEEM-TENDED

THE SUBJECT STOOD OVERLOOKING THE SEA

BUT AS CONCEPT THE SUBJECT WAS THERE ALREADY

yes I accept it

SO IT'S NOT CORRECT TO SAY APPREHENDED

FOR IN FACT THE SUBJECT BOARDED WILLINGLY

yes I accept it initially I was there already

RELIEVED BY WATERY BLUE CATTLE

yes relieved by watery blue cattle

IT FOLLOWS THEN THAT THE SUBJECT IS NOT

ATOMICALLY ESTABLISHED

I accept that if you cut me I do not bleed

IT FOLLOWS THEN THAT THE SUBJECT IS A HOLE MADE OF STUBBLE

no that is not true there is a limit

I SAY THE SUBJECT IS A HOLE MADE OF STUBBLE

yes I accept it I'm a hole made of stubble

IT FOLLOWS THE SUBJECT IS A HOLE MADE OF STUBBLE

LEAVING A WHITE PRODIGIOUS COLOR

GIVEN TO PERSISTENT MOTHERS HELD TOGETHER BY VENTURING

INTO THE HOLE I HAVE ACQUITTED MYSELF FROM MAKING

SERENITY PREDICTABLE EXCLUDING THE CIRCLES

WHERE THE PENCHANT TO FUSE LIGHT WITH MEAT

SEPARATES YOU FROM BEINGS ATOMICALLY ESTABLISHED

yes I accept it I have no former state

///

+ + +

The feelers say I was taken to bring equilibrium
and the very same need forced them to breathe
me into paintings around the fall of France
surviving mainly on ice and a few figs a day
brought the second stage the two long receding
stripes carried me throughout the paintings I began
to jump controlling the winds and dreaming tall
orange flames pouring over the cities rehearsing
below they say I was only an initial character
guided by six perfected hands and organs working
freely even in death I was led by design past filters
and possible outcomes enriching their circle giving
it shape but also testing the city for its underground
surface had not yet been fully conceived only
partly apprehended it needs a solid agent working
freely yes making Julia's acquaintance but never
on Earth would we have allowed you to plumb
Julia for yourself leaving the city folding her wings
it was beginning the white dot placing its matter

+ + +

The slope here is gradual
and orange
the living aspect a living vault
still the salt of so many others
made it confusing what happens
at any moment
what glare pulsing as spears
through slots in the wood
the horses
on their coats I promise
never to take one for myself
folding her behind my cuirass
all warmth all reflection and on
my heart a great love for the book
for it might change Julia
into an island capable of holding
as many ships as she can
until she herself is the island's
freed ringlet of ships

+ + +

Sometimes do I wonder is Julia a rethought
sensual being feigning nature eclipsing smell
thinking each part of me was imported here
the dilemma retrieving indigenous strains
a wide spread festoon naked figures all repeating
the same aspect same ram-basting population
in service to others I saw them inside lindrical
patterns they give new meaning to the aster
shown to his eye to his eye's black recess
independent of spring there's new life in the study
an attractive newcomer she's a building
but with her clothes off you wouldn't know it
there's war in the east side of the building
inspired in part by my own spring temperament
and observers they make use to stay equivalents
and me to find what space does away with

+ + +

I'm just someone caught up in the need for air
an avid I invite breathing and newcomers on days
we can measure completely sober like a bay rounded
I accept there are bays but are they transparent
transposing do they easily amount to a bay providing
each cell is essentially new both arrangement
and composition put down as measure it means cell
before it means glass in the extreme after nearly
nine visits no change no growth enough of your itinerant
clothing I want to see your highness gratified enormously
but in the way your instinct for human keepers means
I want more human keepers this facility is bony
no one is kissing quick adopt me I'm a seaside holiday
building I have a natural ability with brushes brushing
brings emphatic newcomers to the attention of my body
which one I don't know there's only sixteen counting
so far and I'm not even counting density counting
which body would you choose it's your command
when I gave you three you wanted four I thought
the discussion was about making a man yes that's fine
actually having access to either way means a lot
of manufacturing on two fronts possibly more in a big
space like this we can get away with doing a man

+ + +

Trying to coordinate with the keepers
I'm not a scheming ray on the sea
nor a basic consequence reduced to gold
finding the focus switches the pulse
landing unseen and scalding the city
whose name is synonymous and raising
the matter should each one need feeding

+ + +

I was having a difficult time vetting a man
known through several tiers he was committed
he could bring alerted matter directly to the mind
and sign the words WE ARE ALL HERE IMPORTANT
we salve creation it found us the hidden 400 norths
shouting KILL KILL AND DESTROY but I could never
escape feeling as though I blew a side of Julia like
during the interview I was feeling cold for she left me
out here with the cradles and the soldiers and it feels
like tonight I might not get taken back in like tonight
the dew on my visor comes seeping in and that clouds
pass without happening to sound but are the same
sounds leaving an opposite trace

+ + +

The halls for the most part
held grasses from way back
and on the walls open fields
without hedges thickest
to the southeast and orchards
so the intakes occur
year round by strings of solitary
observers all moving at a time
the waterways arable and clean
and yet that nightingale taste

+ + +

The music onboard sickens at night
this from me who can see music planting
a skull along all the cow paths lining Helsinki
the royal palms there draw water by first
considering the forecast how much the others
might drink then there's the washing all those
newcomers most likely they won't ever find its
one cathedral you enter by wetting your finger

+ + +

Respect the candles listen to the one guitar
passing its hands through all the damp hair
surveying Helsinki a new plastic satchel is loving
the nook where it lies in shadow in hay protecting
the mirror from this one impatient girl holding
her breasts up to the mirror she thinks LAST TIME
THIS MADE YOU WAKE UP and as if music ever did
play in Helsinki the mirror could hear what the girl
was thinking or that inside the mirror lives another
girl brandishing but without light she grows older
hearing light slap at the mirror she hears light slap
at the lantern slaps from the bathhouse we all have
our different slaps at the mirror some contiguous
some baleful but still the same slapping at the mirror
and with both horns wrapped around her
a group of us hearing becomes her smell maturing
as it does into a lake-home climb where the royal palms
there draw water she grows older learning to stab
at the trance she is in I suppose in that way it becomes
her the light the light I never could wrap my head around
not wearing a dress of black sand and flooding the room
with the sand and so another sense develops acutely
it thinks it might compensate the girl who believes she
has not yet been visited twice until holding her breasts
up to the mirror she cries out as though giving an order
a white dot would obey I pluck one from the candles
and let it bask that way in the room where it patiently
watches and waits until it decides the mirror should
open now releasing a ram

+ + +

Those rangers trained in the marsh
grew even taller and their variety
aroused me it was explicit making
long rich sorrowful yells
along with the adders the gathering
of figs compressed them just singing
to the mountainous bees to their sable
interiors to their own bees sizing
inside what thunderous vim what bees
of hark and hurry and seasonal drift
given to this one starlet granted
a complete zombie nine months a year
still she did make promising demands
shouting JUST HOW MUCH HERODOTUS
GETS EATEN DOWN HERE ANYWAYS
it was a difficult spring seeing her working
the beast and all that yarrow in the pen
to this day she insists was never her

+ + +

In wind the ship rose questions
to the noise was it the wind you had
come back to see or was it the wind
feeding you thoughts to have asked

+ + +

Behind the eyelets of her netting
both nipples gambol freely and
enjoy tall decade wrought baths
lounging about yellowing gardens
I was made to skate upon one naked
and with concave sandal purpose
slicing my thumb for the scoundrel
it was finally admitting there exist
actual women livids but disguised
as gaming tables they have anxious
parrot like movements setting out
as common folk moving gladly
to the next fortified city committed
to a single post looking downward
having it out with blood and stars

+ + +

At times between us just warming my hands
at one of the tines I felt there was a root thirst
between us caught between slow fast and yet
to occur a lightning cull to my head split in two
I was growing tired and surviving as spectators
we cannot marvel or possibly enjoy each other
in that way forever one blinks then the other

+ + +

I'm feeding her now quick
she's onto my other hand
casting it out for all its pitiful
fires leaving it out for several
statements going down to what
the mingled orders call half-
lost merely visible and all her
proximate futures calling my
dripping head a bulky puppet

+ + +

We were never to discuss it or perceive it
why even to mention it in dream meant
death by expulsion but now I must speak
it I have too much inventory as they say
I am afraid my body will not convey so
let us melt as two rocks of pink flake
wrapped in the same seal and crammed
inside a place on your person but where
did you hide it I need to hear you say it you
went to the gate you chose a place to put it
you tell me where you put it alright then
I can't do this you don't understand none
of us were allowed to think it but now all
I do is think it please just share a bit even
a little snowfall helps me feel beautiful

+ + +

Invested as they say YES that's what I've been saying
we have this time together yes that's what I do here
and a good blond tandem hauling in place my god
this is pure it reminds me of Julia's herrick none of us
were allowed to see it once I did see it I was working
this bad observer unnatural pallors he was lurking
to impress me he would say anything did you know
Julia keeps her own herrick it has the balls of a horse
but the face on a girl and such round eyes openly
staring imagine all nature forced to stare inside a span
Julia's geyser writhing in hair and on the geyser
said to spout there Julia in all her sickness sat fixing
the quickening mirror from sixteen warring shades
dealings and bountiful deaths my god he went on
like this for as they say a good horizonless while

+ + +

After our business he had me so heated up I went
down to do some observing on my own but never
was a comer less prepared to see what I saw that I let
out a gasp a gasp as they say Christ had ears to hear
for the herrick was real and certainly it heard me
for it swung full round and with Julia engorged upon it
lurching towards me it left trails of new feelers mouthing
behind it and of its six teats three swung partly severed open
so the feelers could feed there and with half-turning change
into hair they were feeding on hair and that actual human
face so openly staring that I could not grovel to it or pass
through its last chance salted phases but the glutton Julia
had become her breast distended and buckling like a barge
so overloaded with shades I eventually came to calling it Hell

+ + +

But what a pleasant leather diamond this barge is
wind-swept and warm and babied by tresses

+ + +

I cannot tell you anything more about Julia's herrick
for one thing she wasn't that horrible and Julia didn't
treat her that badly it was just that the herrick was still
only a girl and though it's clear now Julia adored her
treating her to wrens and fish and the like even on occasion
visiting the stations where her people once failed her but
the herrick was essentially Julia's prisoner and as the feelers
piled up the herrick's film grew more pronounced and more
than one observer remarked how the whole ship seemed
distracted the clearing confounded pristine samples mixing
with stock a breakout of shingles that could have been avoided
a few runaways one that never came back and so great was
the depth in her eyes for their part avoiding my gaze and nearly
the pull from the feelers it seemed to me Julia left too much
to the feelers after only six studies already they controlled
all aspects and the abandon and navigation Julia entrusted
to the feelers made me arnica nervous there was one season
all we did was sleep inside a clear access the feelers were free
to reconnoiter and reconnoiter they did for when the order
was given to awaken the itinerary was already set and where
was Julia as always riding her herrick and wearing a garland
of shriveled chimps and perching listlessly on a mast on a rafter
on a dock the colored beam was her virescence depleted and gun
blue like a planet contesting its air or that blackening on a face
a human face the first time loading its feeler

+ + +

There was a time during the first two studies
before things got so heated deliberate and tense
and though the sensation was forbidden
and in most cases blank I can still recall slightly
this gold pioneer spirit moving freely about the ship
and thinking for itself and the little ones their genuine
excitement learning more husbandry than we could
imagine and sailing together in time when Julia still
considered her young and was given to fawns as much
as she was to the older ones and sending each ranger
on holiday partly for respite and partly to track tag
and impregnate as many samples conditions on Earth
would allow and though now it seems dated sentimental
and slow at the time it worked perfectly fine imparting
life to the rangers whose tendency when left alone
when not given concrete projects concrete goals
was to masturbate constantly spilling more seed than you
would think was physically allowed a single month's
worth for example could fill all the cathedrals in Spain
I know this because once I saw this exactly happen once
there were three rangers wintering together in yarrow
some light study yes but also on occasion they'd go out
dressed up as brash Catalan characters but the town
would have nothing of it and of the few women they did
manage to sample one was an old man another hopelessly
barren and the third I think there were three she had
one of those asphodel murmurs so that one night years
later the ranger admitted she died long before he had

finished and I can tell you it took much holiday for that
ranger to feel himself again he needed friends the drinking
the shouting and forcing of hymns together spraying
the beards the braids and like so much mindless paper
clogging the streets it nearly brought Julia's attention so white
were the streets it reminded me of our one full size disaster
when a newcomer entirely on purpose turned over some tables
and Julia come swooping and killing and shredding the hood
she wore in those episodes when the herrick refused to receive
her when all space seemed filled with this stuck mandible silence
a silence even the highest feelers knew not to think

IV

+ + +

Enough time since I was born had passed that the great
domes of chariot flight fell to my hand one was named Julia
but not before I knew her and could slip down to her
such stars of eager distress that I leave it for you to decide
whether she lit out from the very beginnings and along
with her saddle actually did rhyme with the first
shout of the day still in my boyhood she appeared heated
intensely heated and wearing a bauble of decorative gasses
and never having to say we each travel at the speed of our
own awareness and directly to the spot that can serve it
at what point would a spirit willingly not choose biting a curtain
it began to rip ripping the words who exactly allows it to be said
from what moment do there exist rooms of disquieting bodies
all conforming to the same aspect that it became required
to invent distribute then finally exhaust my own budding
command a variety of shape substances and what light there
was no need to cry out so full was her highness that absolutely
the words of the bard suited her well she did not seem to be
a hummingbird from any planet but rather a fledgling craft
in nascent flight and about her body which I freely admit
to removing from underground and to concealing on my person
even now between velocities a single lie is all it needed
she is fake all I do is sometimes blow upon her

+ + +

Such vehemence that of course it made for an outside vehicle
the hulled planet distilled to a plume and from the exhaust
enough time had past that finally a hummingbird appeared
on the sky with the living girth of a city it happened ok
I was banded by an officer I was standing by the sea at a railing
the evening showed me to its hand a stadium where there are no
people only stray white garlands rousing the hand and stammering
and perforations and yes yes we can make you into a cloud of living
man LOOK DIRECTLY AT US all I could see was Julia's farm-boy
face only just bigger than a cupola and gleaming like an oarsmen's
other side grin but also singing the terrible song of hunted lands
she perched above me slowly ripping a spaniel and forcing the white
candies into my body I ascended on a slap into fortified rooms
passing closely was the first time breathing into a room but what
vehemence her sable like a crushed time machine slowly being fixed

+ + +

Hunting men for food and pleasure
escalating changes in ice and land
gradually confused men for their heat
until eventually they were THE HEAT
allowing me but not really allowing
me the freedom to redo the whole flat
as you enter the feeling is you enter
the instep along a bog some serene
people are sleeping there and living
peacefully as greenery a soft central
candied light a fountain bog system
some pink ragged gloamings but light
totally unobtrusive and these subtle
long natural quiets if the flat did have
a clock Time was the clock's appliance
but never did it play any role destroying
the feel of the place where as often as
not I sat there paying out thought
to the nature of things

+ + +

The travagant white tip of a nurse
Adonis spooning a raptor I saw this
once peaking through a slit in the kiln
and hearing the bog calling all marshes
calling all marshes but in a voice not
its own another green ceramic bell
sat still glazed with the game slaughter
exciting white vision if not for the fact
there arrives far enough from the drop
the most innocent crumpled little bell
made to sleep a bell's blackened city sleep
and all the candies break apart so white
white as in the white powder is white
or when divining a dress openly buried
in powder the bell lay sleeping there rasping
waken me gently brushing my back
and with the suicide calming inside
at the end she did agree to give us her heat
but the bell began to tighten and worry
all the young pearl like fawns spooking
for real now as they piled up at the gates

+ + +

To feel each privilege taken away
the first wind-blown animal songs
the painting as evidence the night
and day virgins advancing toward
life their customary sounds happily
gnawing a lake the lake hearing what
the lake can tell libations in triumph
softening dancers enjoying the tables
where newcomers can talk and spray
even so loving the spray for the fight
the taken to the moment the study
the sky no scaffolding can hold
looking towards the end of a season
a new friend in total conquest all her
forbidden ways so precious to the eye
lounging for a spell just not drinking
from the one good tear it could make

+ + +

To be blamed for so much having gone
wrong the slow failure of glass put back
as a future continent a ray bearing rock
blinding some rangers still in training
they wandered for years along the black
fumes of venomous naught such gibbet
eyed warriors but with that orange potable
sill they diluted the mission the blood until
finally they were this blond open killing
force tandem killing now some gamuts
now a courier he got just sort of too much
tagged to death one night they were still
tagging back then and mistook the odd
bastard for one of those stranded poorly
dappled samples and one time some tom-
foolery my ill advised pantomime of Julia
when she was young still so small a mere
butterfly I was doing her first days when
she was still slight and restless all lumbering
after-hatch so rich with the thriverants
all about her were the dead blue-eyed
indigents passing through dunes of their
own flowering it was my idea my motivation
I take the blame but I was only having fun
and it was never meant in mockery or spite
and ever intended as one of those plays
that in the bending scorn the patron

+ + +

The basic outline of my story is evil
Julia was happy living among her
kind each one born under usual light
when there appeared in the distance
two figures splitting the distance
the entire flock took notice seizing
birth weapons and folding insects
and hostile listening devices providing
barbs and violent trickery magic until
the full mask of our intent slid off
making quick egypt rape excursions
unless the hero acts but he does not act
there is no hero no hero exists

+ + +

All night in the cell the bay leaf dripped
until by morning its loud white potion made
an island of my horn and still for some time
it dripped down onto my horn I was said
to have felt it uncoil loosely from my brow
only this time in reverse the boatswain sat
scraping the gristle even tasting the gristle
and forging a miter from the last whorl tracking
inside I was one part aridity one part loam
and began to leave rings gorges and blue tactical
meats this time without council mining a shade
for too much of my horn was now his component
his clear orange centrifuge pattern and looking
rather impatient from the mirror as if I was the one
chosen to say it to tell him look your slow youth
did not bring home to mother her medicine in time
still she can see you sounding the mirror your new
eye fills with the light only just not sporting a horn
and as though she began to understand in the hallway
some boulders appeared and even while she withdrew
deep into that system the boy followed behind
happy as he was that she would now attend to him

+ + +

She started making
these quick little touch-
and-goes abruptly non-
existent she decides she
better investigate the red
scoop for hunting flowers

+ + +

Rays imagine you're a transport
the size of Letuva and you have
standing orders to hide inside try
pulling that off without raising a
flag to the bovine construct of man
she made military observers not to be
gainsaid claiming this orange white
cord to be my savior my fountain
my own white redeeming in blood
white of my leader white by itself
white votives white lips white anything
else YES white prawns white lips white
dot panning the mirrors for white

+ + +

The more involved I became with the study
the more fecund did the study amount to this
poisoned sanctuary where the absence of audibles
in one way made up for the din of infighting
and changing allegiances and all these self-styled
ice-pack vigilantes whose zeal for indigenous strains
put the first real entry point released in a cloud
seeded with cages the cages left open never changing
position Julia floats there in the cage she was in

+ + +

Banished is a strong word let's just say I no longer
feel welcome inside and that now I just can't go
combing any animal any time I want and that Julia's
command no longer seeks my council basically I was
put down in the spot I got taken only now the sea
stares evenly back at me I have the constant anxiety
and the headaches the dreaming a tall white porpoise
and this green swatch of boiled cloth floats above me
when I bathe it watches me sizing inside some idiot
dog skull polished by the green leaves of Brooklyn
to keep quiet she offered me all the nations of the world
and for the ones far off her finger grew and unfurled according
to the curvature of the Earth needless to say it was an endless
and repulsively bony finger the knuckles big as elbows
and pink with prophecy the face on her cock is so intense
and the curvature especially the curvature for it allows me
varying degrees of curvature and turning to my side lets lose
sudden tidal surges and I must be regarded as a snow covered
skiff bashing the island we made with our kiss

+ + +

I cut off my chestnut braid and send it to you
hoping the feel of a chestnut braid in your hands
might give you the picture of a mob cut up by grapeshot
and the genuine chambers of a girl but in the opposite
sense I sometimes have the impression that of the ninety
two hairs comprising this braid two were taken by force
six I lost in Detroit and the rest probably belong to the same
class of person this gulch painter I knew from Madrid
described as an evening ride of pressing stars and deep
pocket asides and there's another impression from the same
period neither peers nor your inclination for rural life
prevents me from saying essentially I'm the world's personal
assistant and while I may prefer simple and direct asking
I'm not opposed to finding a louse on my thigh now and again
nor would I mind sharing your favorite sprite of all time
like testaments yelling one gathers her initial reaction was partly
due to her own warring fingers and not a little to the charms
of a well placed wad my belief right or wrong is that combing
was the first true friend she ever really had in the highest
quarters of a dome where the workman lives and the orderlies
chiefly a phase on the day she was first presented to me I felt
this strong ongoing glance holding me back it was as if I could
speak of freewill from that pat of quiet she left in my hand

+ + +

Julia's reaction against me is worth recognizing
a column to rest in workmen states of trance
appeasing migrating patterns bleed into subjects
undermining something as simple and good
a loving stare crumples immediately it drops
to the level where this painter is showing me
her effort to be more than a bust drizzled in tar
she's wearing a white bodice of common space
I recognize this I seen you wearing this it's a retainer
mining new densities from the eyelets you whiten
inside conducting yourself you had me worked up
you were the one onboard leaning over with a bodice
not pushing the attack you were the one who did not
ask me to extinguish or abruptly direct me to the subject
or slap at the rope bouncing inside me you wore
everything easily accepted that's been your project all
along you're an island retainer surveying humankind's
preoccupation with hair you helped me inside you're
a curious traveler swimming along at a sensitive distance
stripped by all means trail your hair down into my mouth
down a funnel of dancers bathers and real brothel doubt

+ + +

The evidence against people not being tinged
is overwhelming like a pool tingeing under a gale
or a bride feeling tinge just choosing her color
I was obviously brushing against her a sand
dune indication yielding a lace of feeding flowers
with their full gale movements sizing my body
I sometimes arrive inside exchanging heat rations
I'm a female captain with round scented points
I won't darken inside I'm helping them study
I'm part of a long orange line feeding the center
I'm building the wall up with eggs some eggs
won't darken inside yes love I can hear you
making percussive ground clicking noises you're alive
you're an ice sheet in the wind you carry hoses
sediments and just a tinge some headland mulberry
ices and sixty days in some kingdoms even more
carry me carry me in your mouth like the others
I'm not a cloudy season pinching fourteen eggs
at a time nor the cold waves from three devilish
springs but the dutiful red husks before I was born

+ + +

There were a few starlets in the clearing
singled out by a process of wormwood
selection they held interests and cravings
and gestures alike their movements hung
in the air as pure emancipation the cuttings
supplied prophets with legitimate causes
yes bandits but bandits of ubiquity their
nakedness sighed with privation sighed
for itself an entire france of privation
a handshake held throughout the kingdom
even directions sat askance upon a sword
lowing in detail growing older spouting
different patches vestments and garlands
for the ram not saying if they all went alike
to their ends with infinite conduct

v

+ + +

Tonight Julia awakens painting the way our kiss can sound
there's a reticent lilt to her hand as each hastened stroke
gets confused with our own she's painting let the hallway
worry about the hallway she's not painting sounds in a ship
she's painting they began by walking the lawns together
they began without emissaries they began to get specific so far
they are just two smears so it's hard to tell if the hair was left
to reference the painter or in fact just fell where the painting
had seemed seems how we know how seems together with all
forms hues and shades of leaf we fell there fallen and seeming
last night went searching for three city blocks there is no city
not even Helsinki has something to do with itself yet that banner
deploring the length of our fingers as it would not burn bury
nor tear at the fray begun by our teeth I spread it out and bloodied
myself bled until the study can say the banner means nothing
the banner means nothing but the banner remains crown-stiff
and clotting on what little winds set out to appease the manifold
treasons pulled up by the hoist

+ + +

A braid meaning barely a hidden sage fragrance
tumbles unseen from the nape and onto a farmhouse
where someone else is there taking down entirely
personal now we're cooking with contrails information
the face on a savior rattling and black for he visited
all the scenes and he made me out of orange clay a little
fated person in the manger at night voices wash over me
like a figurine like the distressed lettering at the back
of his neck the serifs graze spoon-headed and dig still newer
wells inside the hymnal let the letters constrict in the snow
let the brown bags of luminaria glissade in office light
and if the paper be bloody let that I thread it as sundown
through the aviary net a net is for talking and with a talking
gun I drop down to the town's most prominent Christ
if temperature positions the outcome of many to suggest
temperature positions the many is a half-truth designed
to make women bend to the geyser tradition temperature
takes the lard from a geyser and mothers it into a hat

+ + +

I press my lips to the manger
a mute happiness
the day's opposite walls
and the stars burn without regard

+ + +

I am wanting so badly to dissuade
you of the passage where my body
appears from the quarry headless
and green and as the end of a length
my head no longer feels allowed but
balanced there on the ledge of a stillness
it pretends to be floating there
on the otherwise blunt wing of the wren
but could you please hold me tighter
whispers the head the head they called darling
and reclines even now on the restful side
of the island where my head went entirely
smooth and in places partially smooth

+ + +

The all white thrust of her breathing
leads to a centralized singer traveling
in ships wide and sedentary and drum
thumping bicycle kids lifting the plume
they do seem to be living between two
categories if only their fathers would give
it a rest no matter how magical they think
a device might be the truth is the truth is
they acquired it underground they made
an intrusion like everyone else and now
that we're down here we might as well
examine the mothers and sisters climb
a huge date tree and disappear forever

+ + +

Julia it is now May 31st and with the three
snowflakes from your sweater I'm building
a fortress with serial hatches and a pink venom
stick wards off the monkey-man self-grooming
in the pedestrian tunnel a covert lung if no one
ever uses no one can ever reject just how easy
it would be to slip down here and die without
ever finding my way to another sunken clearing
they would not hire my severed head not even
on a parking meter now that really does seem
out of order ingratiating the city up to my elbow
just for the listening smell your hair truly is fabulous
but by far the greater accident was inserting your own
tribal land of new particulars for the fortresses here
are already involved already fitted with early hand-
locking mirrors and of the three dulcet beauties
you'll meet in Helsinki one descends into sleep holding
your hand she mumbles porn in her sleep the kind
you can listen to and not hear a blouse trailing in
and out among the mallows and all the world's
radiant hair comes together and I can step no leap
upon a huge unbroken horse it happened ok a ship
to the planet had come eating all things seen or heard

+ + +

She enjoys me in the open
she enjoys watching me invisibly walk on grass
we are both sad virgins warbling in a tower

+ + +

In darkness there's a slug coming towards me
dragging its rail of glister and shine the spout
on its eye tapping my chest the white shivery
nets different from lather or rushing to rescue
a maiden the slug smothers me in dogwoods
at play and foamy among the different nets
I'm all bundled up bundled for death I can see
Julia furnishing stars my own understanding
of stars what Julia called THE GREAT DETOURS
climbing outside climbing barefoot a daughter
of the grasses she imagines the guise of my body
but as a baby skimming its mother's breast she
pats me she kisses me she carries me out into a field
and presents me to the night O white swath of all time
a single star just falling then I'm wiggling I'm shiny
I'm that wet newborn from Roots all hope all
promise but with huge accelerating growth until
I'm too huge to even hold and we run off together
making love inside our own locomotive hiding yes
but not with anxiety or the constant clip clip clip
her enormous bush giving me all its power and dread

+ + +

But the star wasn't guiding me at all it was leaving
me I was being left behind I'm that silver oil stick
left out here in the yard all summer a glass boat
but without the boat just great depths of insurgency
I'm in the shallows with a sunlit can of Fanta tall
fronds begging for taller looking down at my patches
I have these competing transparent patches ingesting
my body help me I'm growing quilted all I can see
is the yard with its animals and a tunnel filling my chest
a tunnel with all those different days but days already
apprehended exhausted and I can barely peer down it
I'm coursing through resin or ice or varnish regardless
it's one of those tunnels and I can see there's a man
trudging inside it he's carrying a baby but the baby
looks complacent angry and old the baby barely
moves it's a doll and it looks real familiar it's a doll
a brown bearded muscular doll naked he tells me
to lie down beside him he wants to compare our patches
look we both have these transparent patches eating our bodies
great could you please say it louder I don't think Majestic
heard you go ahead no really it's ok do what you want
show me the glittering strands thicker than a garden it doesn't
matter I'm already being digested by a creature whose glister
I don't understand sobbing a wet living mountain
or practicing woodsmen treason with a GI he's going to great
lengths to make sure the doll in his hand holds a jar of transparent
bearded men dragging behind them the thick bridal gauze
worn between two sisters and wanting to eat yes

but not from a sore in the morning the entire ship can see
I have slippery clear but also stretchy lines crossing my body
crumbly in places my legs slightly gummy slightly damp
and I have my skin in the sun splitting until there is nothing
but a fern patterned nozzle scalding my body and no more
days at the pool or together in the red barn putting on plays

+ + +

In Helsinki there's a club called Timocharis
and a really good nautical band whose primary
sail is the pink and white paper used for packing
meat so we never thought they'd make it past
the outer bank islands let alone that buoy to keep
the swimmers in basically we thought they'd all drown
that it would happen really fast and we would watch it
happen but instead they just sailed away
and they seemed really keyed-up as they sailed away
like a greased melon with red scoops for catching wind
now they live in one of those tents quilted from innumerable
water-colors and batik tablecloths of fond association
and true pacific sofas where they can masturbate to the sound
of fresh greens and scraps of conversation always steering
the subject towards a holy quarter and I can paint them
actually just the bassist sitting alone with his half-empty
decanter of wine or reading aloud from his essay on spirit
tension or just watching him play to his buds in the canopy
and while the tent's strong profusion of masculine binding
may set it apart from the rest of the village as a sheltering
scheme the tent is a failure sunlight and wind passes beneath
and on its anchoring poles the darkness lands in wreaths or hoops
if a flag were attached there the prayers were encoded
black on the inside red on the out at dawn the tent appears
with the sun just upon it like a large orange hide staked
to the ground by three orange feathers I never really did feel
at home in Helsinki one night was so cold I slept beside
a wheezing black dog whose open sores made darkness

and pus the next day I met these three girls from Macedon
who let me stay in their cabin for a week never was a man
more happy and free this is an understatement I mean
these were the kind of girls who knew how to grow
yogurt but also enjoyed shooting skeet in the afternoons
we drank Makers and one night they really did weave
a crown of vetch for me to wear

ABOUT THE AUTHOR

Peter Richards was born in Urbana, Illinois in 1967. He is the author of two previous collections of poetry, *Oubliette* and *Nude Siren*, and a chapbook, *Hibernal*.

ACKNOWLEDGMENTS

Grateful acknowledgment is made to the editors of the following journals who published sections from *Helsinki*: *Advocate: Graduate Center CUNY, Boston Review, Cavalier, Columbia Journal, Crowd, Cutbank, Electronic Poetry Review, Gutcult, Jubilat, Left Facing Bird*, and *Make*.

Several poems from *Helsinki* were published in a chapbook, *Hibernal*, Empyrean Press, 2010.

Thank you to my family and friends for their love and guidance while writing this book. Special thanks to Dr. Godfrey Louis and Dr. Chandra Wickramasinghe whose research on interstellar grains influenced much of this work.